DREAM TIME
THE BEGINNING

"David and Nicole, time for bed," granny said. Bed time is the best time for David and Nicole because granny reads all the stories in the Bible. Granny said it's important to know the truth about the God of Abraham, Isaac and Jacob.

God did so many good things for people. I remember what Granny read to me and my sister Nicole last night. She told us about David and Goliath. David in the Bible wasn't scared of that mean old giant. Granny said I am brave just like the David in the Bible.

Nicole is 4 years old. It's hard for her to stay awake while Granny reads the Bible; especially when she can't take a nap. I'm 6, so I don't have to take naps anymore. I can stay woke the whole day without getting sleepy.

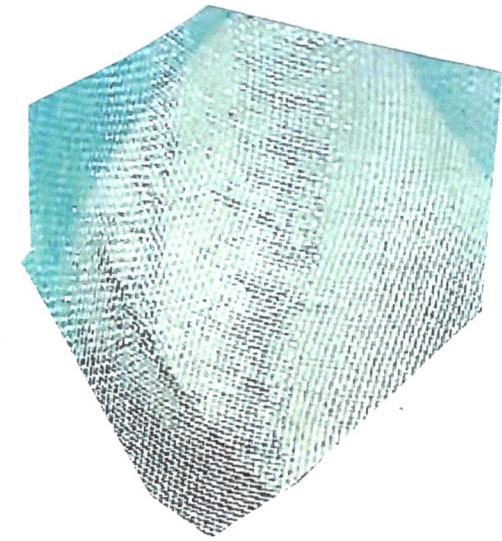

Every time I hear all about the good things God did in the Bible, I have a dream. When I dream, it seems like I am right there in the pages of the Bible. The good thing about my dream is Bear is always with me. Bear is my dog. He follows me everywhere I go.

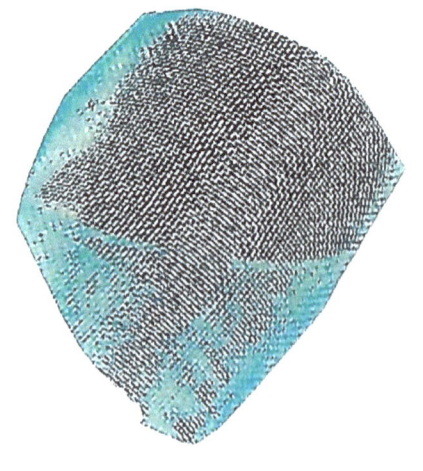
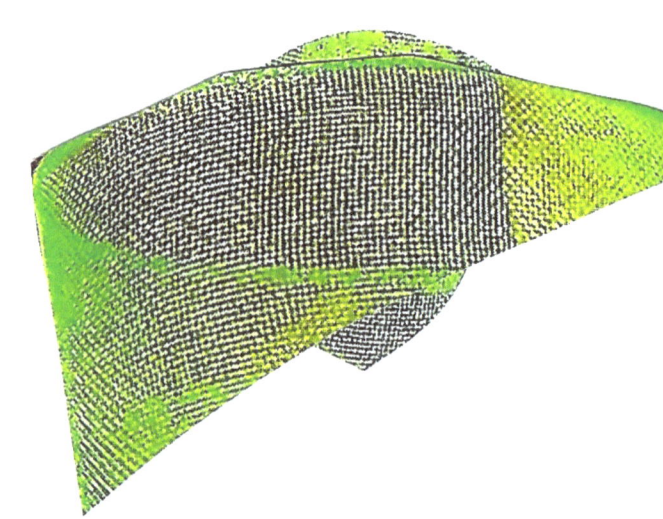

Nicole is there too. She brings her doll Bess because Bess is special. I can't tell you why she's special. Nicole made me promise that I would never tell; so I have to keep her secret.

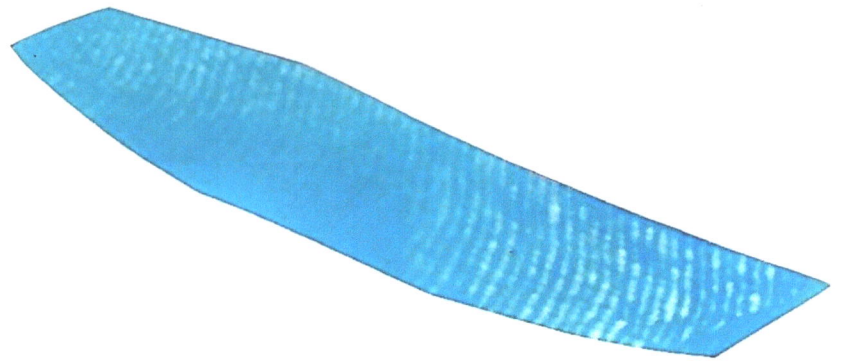

Every time I wake up from the dreams, I learn something new. Granny says that's because God is speaking to my spirit that lives on the inside of me. I don't understand everything about the spirit that's inside me, but I want to know. That's why I always pay attention when I hear granny talking about God.

Nicole starts talking about the things we see from our dreams at breakfast. Even though I know that I'm asleep, I remember everything when Nicole starts talking. I don't know why Nicole can't stay awake when granny reads to us. Nicole remembers everything too. I'm glad that she remembers. I don't want Nicole to grow up and not know all about God. Granny said all people should know about God.

God is so smart. He made everything and he remembers everything he made. He even remembers everybody he made. God remembers all the people all over the world. He must have a good memory like me and Nicole.

"David, tonight I'm going to put Nicole to bed before I start reading so that you can sit on my lap," Granny said. David was shocked. "I'm 6 years old. I'm too big to sit on your lap. I'm not a baby like Nicole," David said. If I sit on granny's lap, she's going to keep kissing my head and squeezing me tight. No, I don't want to sit on granny's lap. Big boys don't sit on their granny's lap.

Granny looked at David and understood. "You know what David; I think you're fine sitting where you are. You're right, you are 6 years old now and that makes you too big to sit on granny's lap," granny said. David smiled and let out a sign of relief.

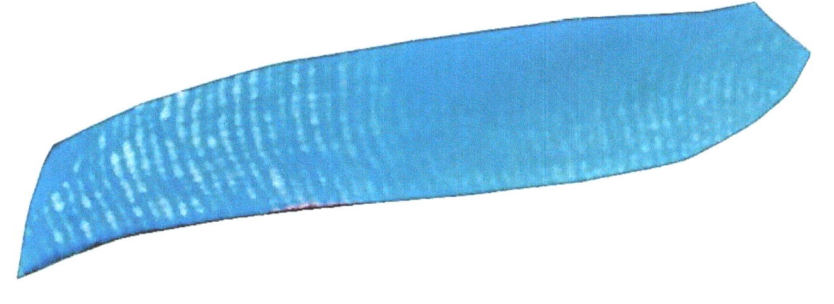

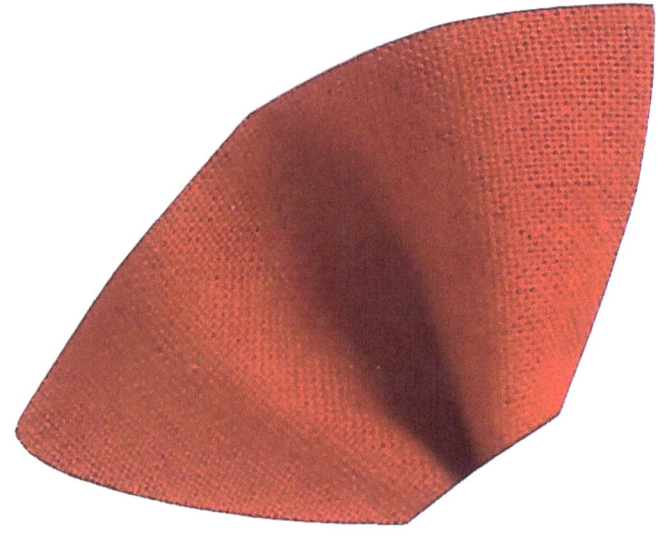

"Granny, can you read about the beginning when God makes everything," David asked.
"Of course honey, I will start at the beginning," Granny said.

"In the beginning, God created the heaven and the earth," Granny said.

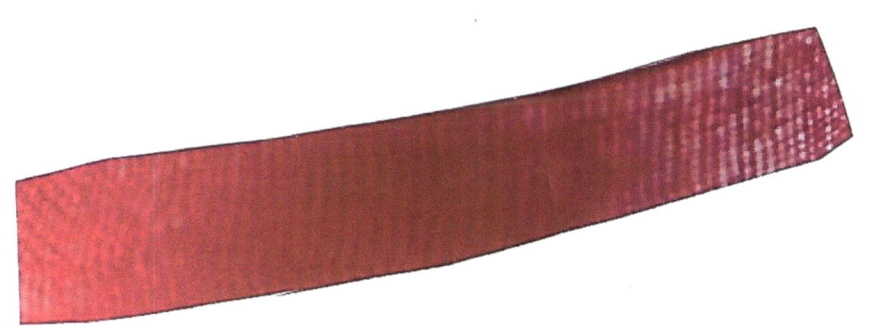

David remembered the first time they heard the voice of God.

David, Nicole, Bear and Bess were standing on a long, red, blue and yellow cloud. They saw two chairs near the cloud. One chair was blue and the other chair was red.

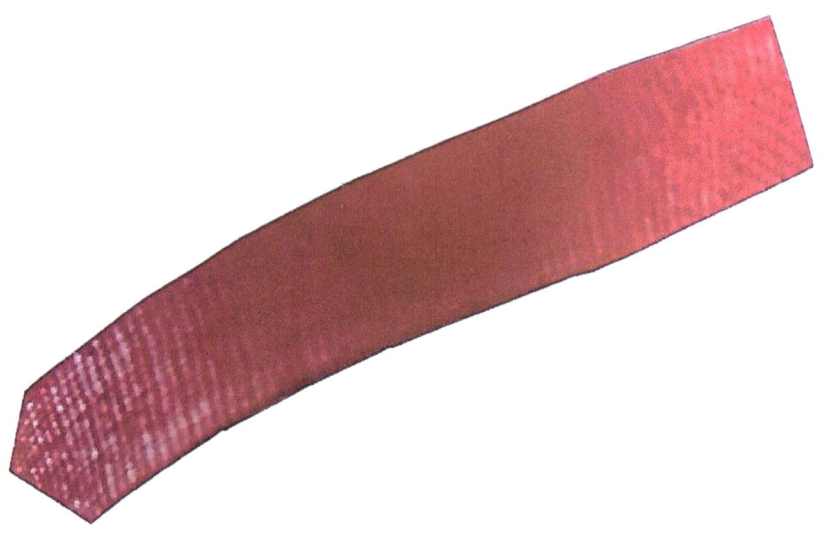

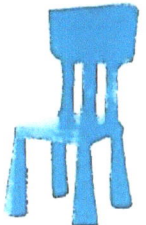

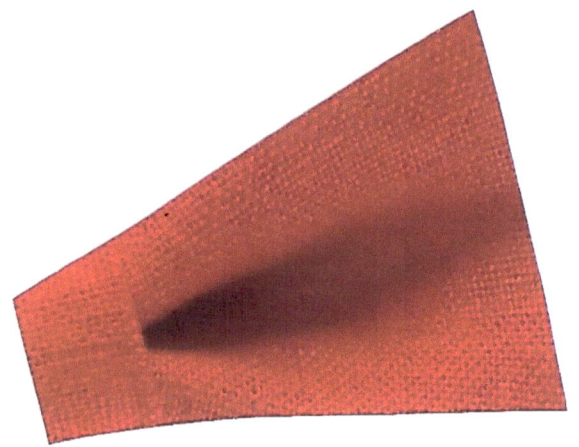

It was so dark. They couldn't see anything outside of the cloud. Nicole began to cry so David held her hand. David could feel Bear climbing on top of his shoe. He must be scared too.

"Nicole, don't be scared. I don't know where we are, but I know we're safe. God will protect us," David said. He was trying to be brave because it was so dark. David had never been anywhere where it was so dark. Even when granny turns the lights out in his bedroom, he can still see when his eyes adjust to the light. And David always has his flashlight under the pillow to look at his baseball cards when he can't fall asleep.

Just then David and Nicole heard a voice. The voice said, "Don't be afraid. I will never hurt you. I love you," the voice said.

The voice continued, "Let there be light!" David smiled because light was everywhere. They looked around, but there was no one in sight. "Who said that," Nicole asked? "I don't know, but at least we can see," David said.

"How come everything's covered with water," Nicole asked. "I don't know, but I hope we find out," David said.

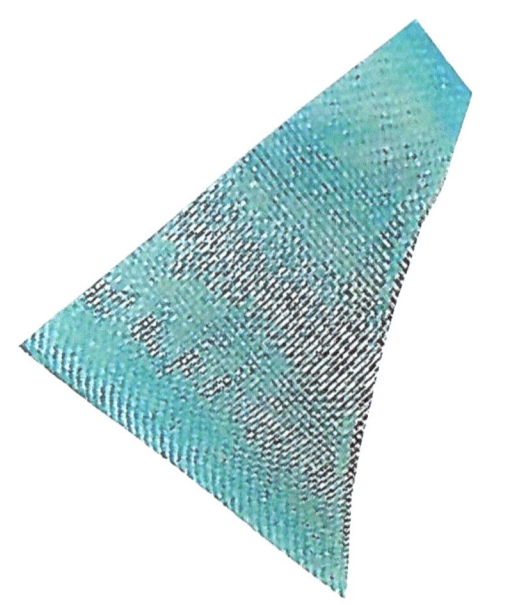

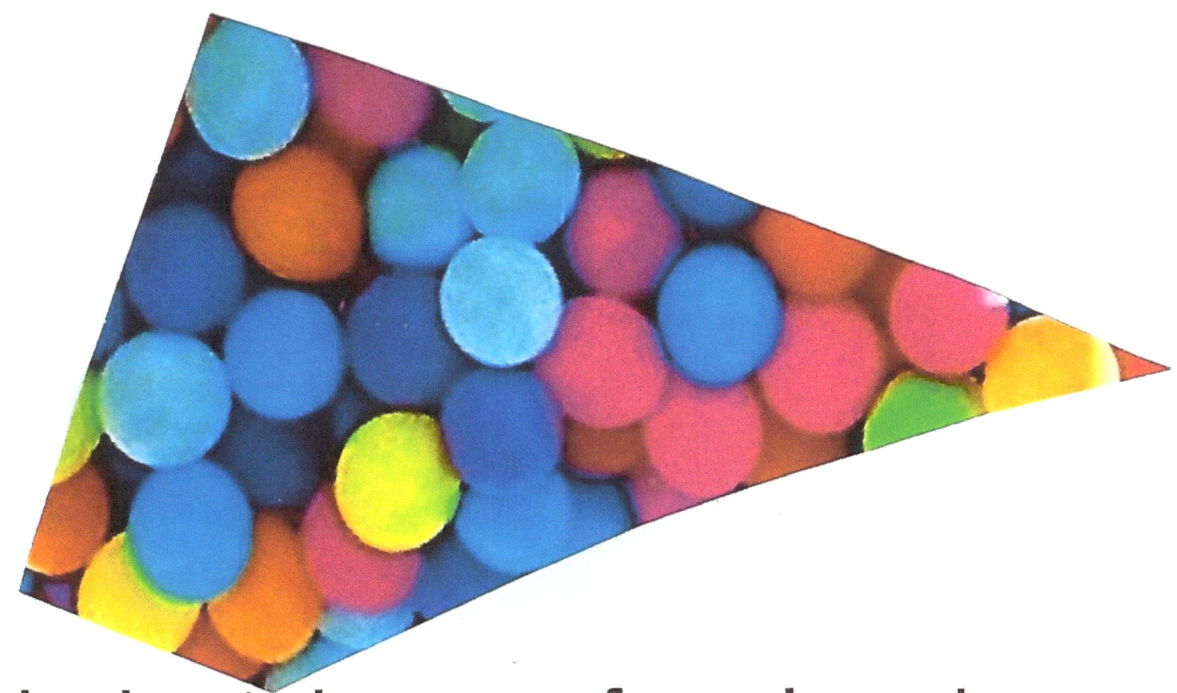

"David, don't let go of my hand. You know I can't swim," Nicole said. "I know you can't swim, and I won't let go of your hand. Sssh, I hear something," David said.

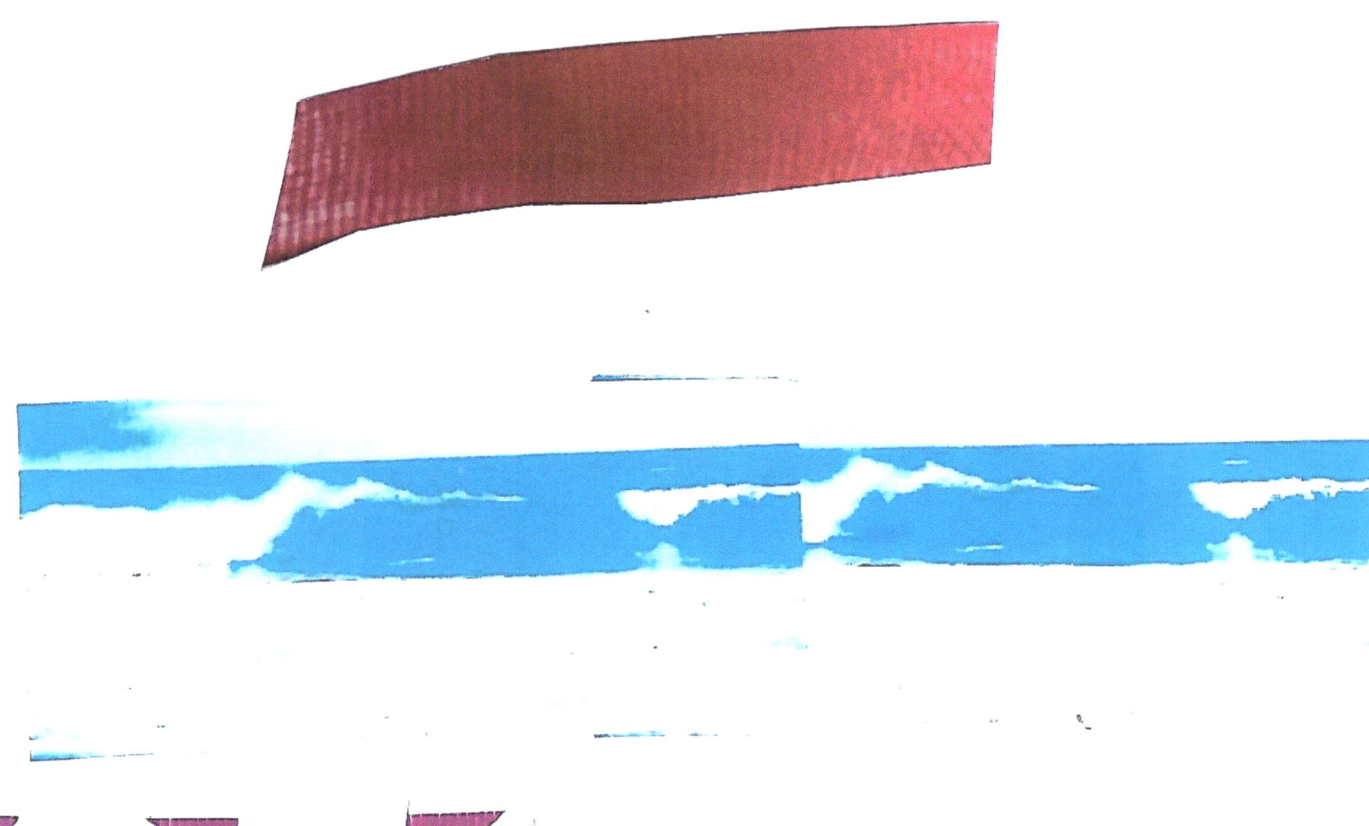

They heard the same voice again. God spoke and made the sky. Then God separated the water in the sky. God made the water in the sky separate from the water under the sky. God named the sky heaven. This was the second time David and Nicole heard the voice, and it was the second time something happened when they heard the voice.

"Who is that and how come they're hiding," Nicole asked.

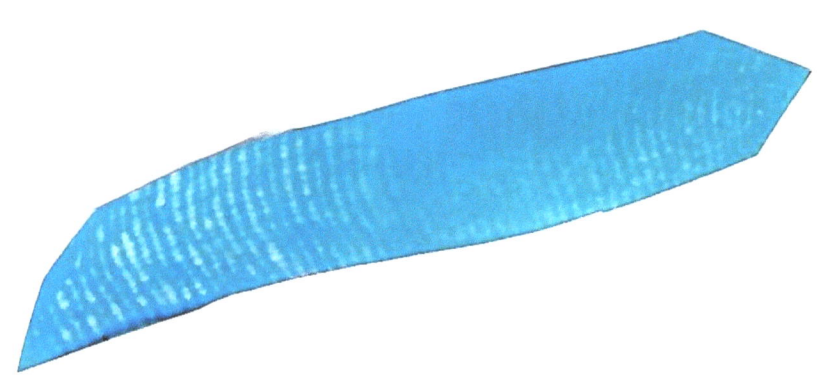

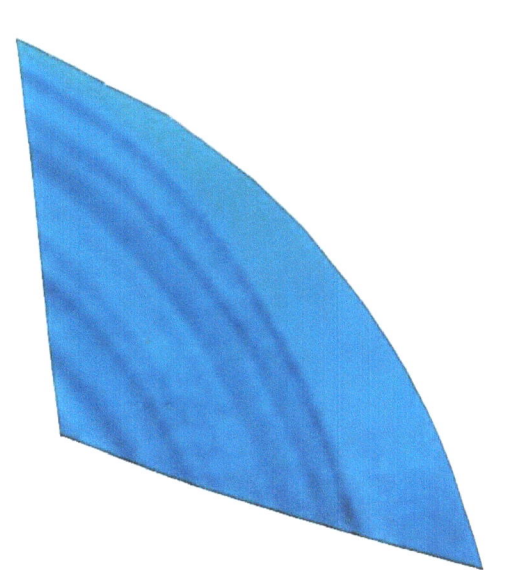

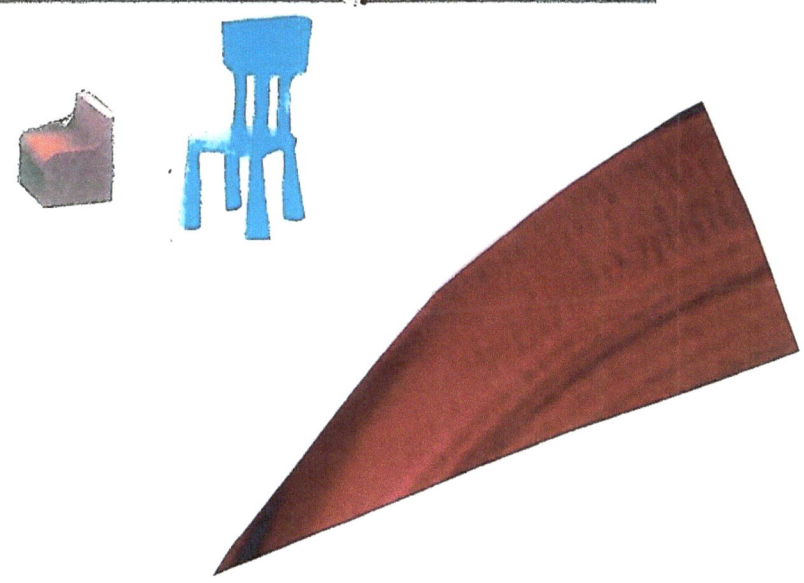

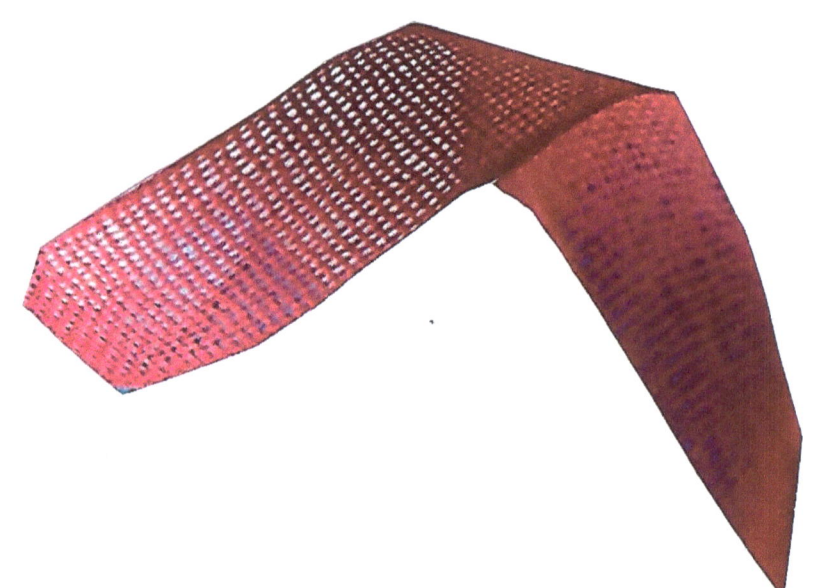

"Who's there," David asked?
"This is God. I brought you here to show you how I made the world in 6 days. I don't want you to see me right now. I want you to see how the world was made," God replied.

"Separate water beneath heaven and go to one place," God commanded. The waters separated as soon as God spoke.

"This is cool," David said.

"Land appear," God commanded. The waters dried up and land appeared just like God said.

"God is making miracles," Nicole said. "Yes, he is," David replied.

God named the land *earth*. He named the waters *ocean*. God saw that it was good.

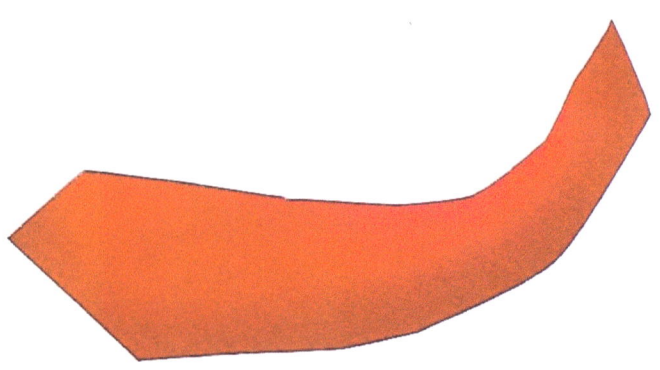

"This is the best," David said.

God spoke again. "Earth, bring forth all types of plants and trees. I want to see grass on the ground."

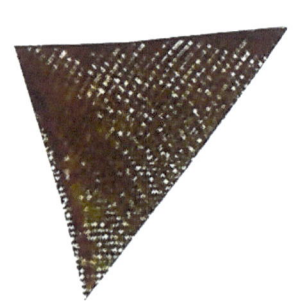

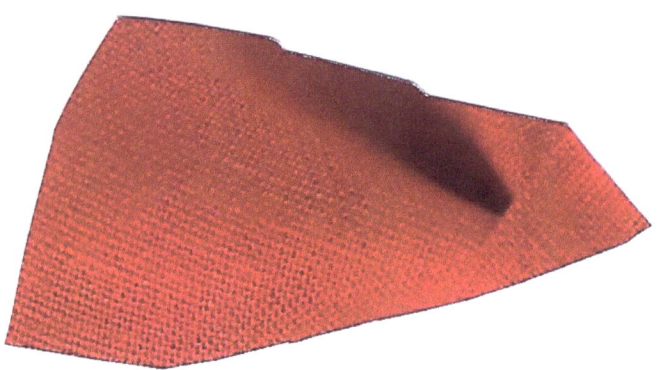

Nicole was scared. She was ready to go home. "Bess is tired and hungry and I want to go home," she said. "I know you're getting tired because you haven't had your nap," David said.

"I'm getting sleepy," Nicole said. "Don't you want to stay to see what God is going to do next," David asked? "Bess is ready to go," Nicole replied. "I think Bess is tired, but she wants to stay so she can see what happens next," David said. "Okay, I'll stay for a few minutes," Nicole said.

God spoke again. "Lights come out and shine in heaven's sky. Separate day from night. Mark seasons for days and years. Light in heaven's sky, I want you to give light to the earth," God commanded.

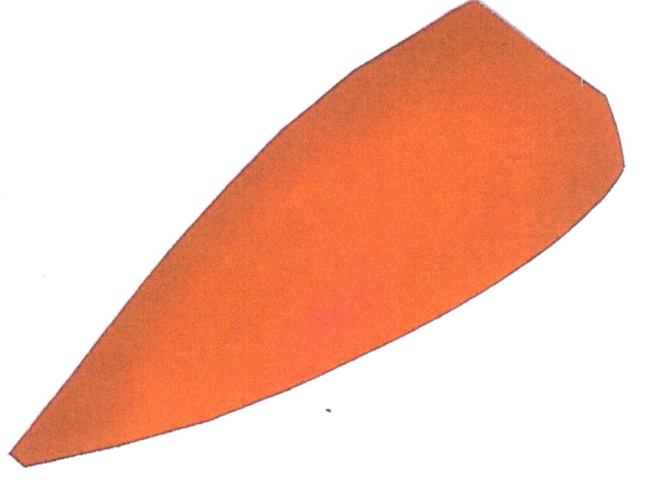

"Wow, that's a lot of stuff that God can do. Who is God talking to," Nicole asked? "God is talking to the earth. He made the earth, and the earth has to do what God says," David replied.

"Remember, we saw those two lights that God made. One was the sun and the other was the moon. God also made stars. He put them in the sky to light up the earth. The sun will shine in the day, and the moon will shine at night," David said.

"God has been real busy," Nicole replied.

God spoke again. "Ocean, I want to see all kinds of fish."

"God said, "Birds fly through the sky all over the earth."

God created the huge whales and everything that lives in the waters.

God saw that it was good. He blessed everything that he made.

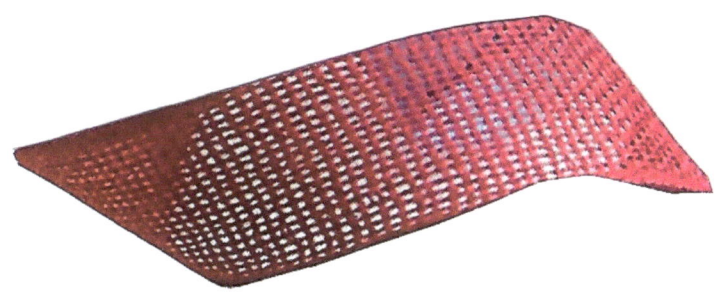

"Hold up your hand Nicole and count your fingers," David said. "One, two, three, four and five," Nicole replied. "That's how many things God created so far," David said. "Do you think He will make five more things, so I can count on my other hand," Nicole asked? "Let's see," David replied.

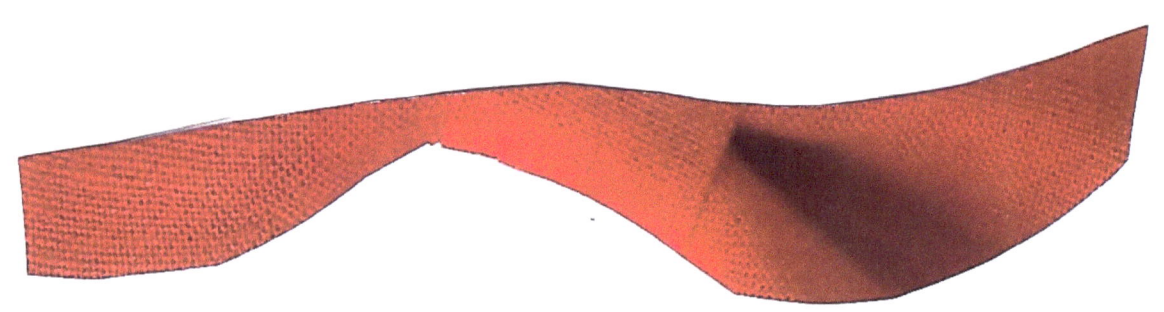

"Earth bring forth life of every kind such as cattle and reptiles and other animals," God commanded. David and Nicole, saw lions, buffalos, zebras and bears. God saw that it was good.

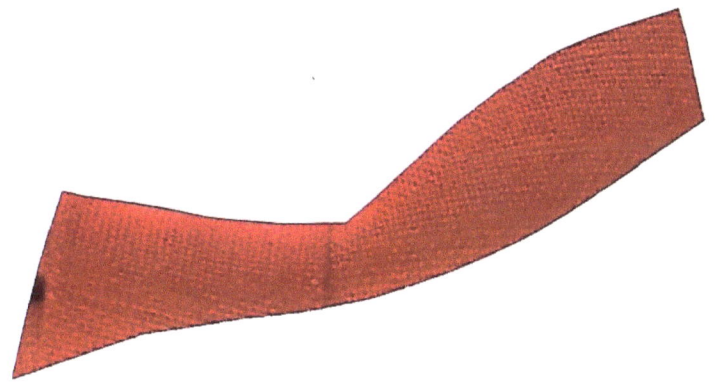

"Look at all the animals," Nicole said. "Nicole, look at the white bear, David responded. "He don't look like Bear," Nicole said. "He's not a dog, he's a real Bear," David replied.

David and Nicole were amazed the animals were not in a cage like the ones they saw at the zoo. "Look, they all love each other," David said.

"I want to go down and play with the tiger," Nicole said. "You can't go play with the tiger," David responded. "Why not," Nicole asked? "Because we can't get off this cloud," David said. "I want to play with the tiger. Me and Bess are going to get off this cloud so we can play with that tiger," Nicole insisted. Nicole started to walk towards the edge of the cloud when God spoke again.

"Let us make a man and a woman in our image and likeness. Let us make them to act like we do. They will look like we do. The man and woman will be responsible for the fish in the sea. They will command the birds in the air. They will also command the animals on the ground. They are going to be responsible for everything that I created on the earth," God said.

"Look at those people down there with the animals. I wish I could go down there with them," Nicole said.

"Nicole, you have me, Bess and Bear to play with. God brought us here to see all the good things he did when he made the world," David said.

David and Nicole looked at each other. They both started to laugh. They laughed so hard their tummies ached.

www.ingramcontent.com/pod-product-compliance
Lightning Source LLC
Chambersburg PA
CBHW060758090426
42736CB00002B/74